Unapologetically Me

Also by
MARIA R. PALACIOS

The Female King

Karate on Wheels: A Journey of Self-Discovery

Criptionary: Disability Humor & Satire

The Goddess in This Woman: A Journal for the Woman's Soul

The Girl in This Goddess: An Empowerment Journal for Girls and Young Women

The Big Little Black Book: An Address Book Revealing What Women Want Men to Know

Dressing Skeletons: A Poetic Tribute to Frida Kahlo

Poetic Confessions: Volume I

Poetic Confessions: Volume II

Unapologetically Me

Empowerment Affirmations for People with Disabilities

By Maria R. Palacios

Atahualpa Press, Houston, TX

Carrying a Heavy Gift

Be it a tribute to the first to fall,
Or a final salute to those who still stand tall,
This dedication is to legacy and to those who feel its call.
...
We'll never forget you, and we love you all.

~ C. H Goodrich

Unapologetically Me

You are perfect and complete just the way you are.

Empowerment is what happens
when we realize we have what it takes
to make a difference ... and we choose to do so.

Never stop referring to yourself
or to your body
with terms of love and affirmation.

Forgive those who've treated you poorly.

Forgive yourself.

Live a life of freedom.

Recount the struggles and heartaches you've survived. It may surprise you to see how strong you really are.

True beauty has little to do with the body
and everything to do with the soul.

Living fully and completely
means accepting and celebrating
the changes that come.

If we choose to stay engaged in life,
the hunger of the soul
will become more and more insatiable!
Feed it!

Aim for greatness,
for you are capable and worthy of it.

MARIA R. PALACIOS

No disability, no boundary, no obstacle ...
can clip the wings of those who want to soar.

UNAPOLOGETICALLY ME

You don't have to be anything but yourself
in all your unique and wonderful ways.

Choose to see yourself as a survivor
even if the world paints you as a victim.
Eventually, they'll get it right.

Disability *is* part of the story –
an *important* part of the story –
but not the *whole* story.

The word "DISABLED" now stands for:

Daring

Independent

Strong

Aware

Beautiful

Lovable

Empowered

Diverse

There is an awesome sense of freedom
that comes from accepting oneself.

We must learn to see ourselves through the lens of love,
for only then will our personal power become evident –
to ourselves and to the world.

UNAPOLOGETICALLY ME

Your life is ALWAYS worth living.

You have something unique and beautiful
to give to the world.

Don't let past failures
define the outcome of your dreams.
Keep trying.

Happiness is about celebrating life

as we are living it!

It is not that you are strong *despite* your differences.
You are strong *because* of them.

It is through Love that we renew ourselves

day to day

and quench the thirst of the soul.

Disability does not equal inability.

Empowerment comes, in part,

from the understanding of this.

You never cease to be a whole person,
no matter what changes the body might endure.

Celebrate your differences every chance you get.

You are worthy of Love.

When we make peace with the body,
we make peace with the world.

Experience can only bring us wisdom
if we are willing to learn from our mistakes.

Don't let others define
what independence means to you.

MARIA R. PALACIOS

Don't measure your dreams with an able-bodied ruler.

Dare to just be YOU,

in all your unique and awesome ways.

Avoid using negative statements
about yourself or your body.
We tend to eventually believe EVERYTHING
we tell ourselves.

Give yourself permission
to experience your feelings and mourn your losses.
It doesn't mean you're weak; it means you're human.

The power of your thoughts
creates the energy you project.
Choose to project empowerment,
for *that* is who you really are.

MARIA R. PALACIOS

Your soul can only know freedom
when Love controls your actions.

MARIA R. PALACIOS

Your soul can only know freedom
when Love controls your actions.

36

You have the *right* to make choices about your own life.

Your inner advocate is alive and well.

You have nothing to be ashamed of,
and a *lot* to be grateful for.

It is up to you to use your abilities
toward positive change.

A disability doesn't mean you can't do something.
It simply means you do your own version
of that "something," and you do it *your* way.

Never doubt that your voice can make a difference.

Empowerment begins with YOU!

Even if doors close on you, or some don't even open,
don't stop knocking.
Eventually one will open,
leading you to exactly where you need to be.

You are a natural source of positivity,
but only if you allow yourself to be.

MARIA R. PALACIOS

There is nothing more liberating than forgiveness,
but especially so as it relates to our bodies.

Turn anger into advocacy.

Choose to channel your frustrations

toward generating hope and the energy of change.

MARIA R. PALACIOS

Believe in yourself
and your dreams will grow wings of their own.

Practice saying "I love you" to yourself,
and *really* mean it.

Confidence comes from your ability
to be comfortable in your own skin.

Believe that you can, and you will.

Don't be afraid to let others know
when something they say is offensive.
Not doing so disempowers *you*
and keeps *them* from potential growth.

Even when we think we have nothing to give,
there is ALWAYS something we can do,
something we can offer, something we share.
Always!

Being disabled often means having to
build our own opportunities.
We must equip ourselves with the tools
to be able to do so.
Knowledge is, indeed, power.

Purposely look for good things
in yourself and in other people.
You might be pleasantly surprised.

You don't owe others inspiration
just because you have a disability.
You have the right to be an average human being,
striving for your own success.

Any chance you get to educate others, take it!

Switching the focus from scarcity to abundance
will open channels of opportunity
you might otherwise miss.

Don't let others define your abilities.

Only you can do that.

Letting go of the things you can't control
will lead you to the things you *can* and *should* control.

You have *everything* you need
to give and receive Love.

What you tell yourself
is more important than what others think of you.

Empowerment is not about trying to look less disabled,
but about maximizing our abilities
and accentuating the power of our uniqueness.

Your life is sacred and worthy of Love.

You hold the key to your own destiny.

True miracles seldom transform the body
but always transform the soul.

Plant a seed of empowerment and watch it grow.

Your abilities are unique and beautiful.

When you feel like running away,
do so to the safety of positive thoughts.

Focusing on your abilities
enhances them and magnifies them.

Reach as high as you can ... and then get a ladder!
There is nothing wrong with seeking help
to empower ourselves to reach higher.

Sharing the power keeps it going.

There is no shame in being disabled,
but it is a shame that some may believe it to be so.

When opportunity doesn't come to us,
we have to create it.

Advocacy is the force that moves mountains.

Don't let anybody suggest that your life
could have more value if you weren't disabled.
It might be easier in some ways,
but never more valuable.

What you have to say matters.
Your *life* matters.

Obstacles are advocacy lessons waiting to happen.

There is no room for pity,
just love and empowerment.

Believe in the transformative energy of self-love.

Empowerment is a muscle
that needs to be constantly exercised.

There is something so powerful
about the realization of our own abilities.

Dreams and plans are important,
but without goals, they will not materialize.
Set goals, and remind yourself
that every single journey begins with one step.

MARIA R. PALACIOS

The word "GIMP" now stands for:

Generally

Independent

Multi-talented

Person (or People)

84

You will find what you're looking for.

It might not be the exact version of what you planned,

but it will be exactly what you need.

The heart can see what the eyes don't.

The glass refills itself through the power of Love.

MARIA R. PALACIOS

It is never too late to act on your dreams,
even if it means creating an adapted version of them –
one that fits your abilities and your means.

Your abilities, your passions, and your dreams
all need to be nurtured.
Doing so will make your spirit soar.

Never let the obstacles of the world deter you from pursuing the desires of your heart.

Dare to see yourself
through the lens of empowerment.

Don't let fear paralyze your dreams.

Define independence not by the things you can do without help, but by the quality of life you can accomplish *with* help, assistance, and support.

MARIA R. PALACIOS

When you need a source of strength, look around;
find it in your peers and in those
who've already been there.

Whether we know it or not,
we are constantly writing and rewriting our own stories.
Choose to share *your* story
from a position of empowerment.

If people stare at you,
stare right back!

YOU are beautiful!

YOU are wonderful!

Dare to be, unapologetically, YOU!

About The Author

Maria R. Palacios is a poet, author, spoken word performer, motivational speaker, social change advocate, disability rights activist, and workshop facilitator. Featured on numerous local radio shows and podcasts, nationally syndicated programs, and in many international publications, Maria's impact on the rights of children, women, people with disabilities, and the Hispanic community is as immeasurable as her artistry is undeniable.

Some of Maria's most cherished accomplishments and positions include her participation in efforts that led to the passage of the Americans with Disabilities Act of 1990, being inducted into the Hispanic Women in Leadership Hall of Fame in 1996 and receiving the Hispanic Excellence Award in 1997, being a member of the International Guild of Disabled Artists and Performers since

2009, exploring her personal connection to Frida Kahlo through live performances of her poetry at Houston's annual Frida Fest celebration for seven straight years, participating in the Gulf Coast Poetry Tour (2009), and creating a publishing company (Atahualpa Press) which has produced nine of her own titles to date, as well as two by other artists with disabilities.

Of particular passion to Maria is Sins Invalid, a performance project of artists with disabilities. With this group she has performed since 2007, co-facilitated their Tongue Rhythm Multi-Disciplinary Poetry Workshop in 2008, and is featured in the 2013 documentary, *Sins Invalid: An Unashamed Claim to Beauty in the Face of Invisibility.*

In the artistic world, Maria is known as "The Goddess on Wheels."

palaciosmaria66@gmail.com

Made in the USA
Middletown, DE
06 May 2021